SCARY STATES (OF MIND)

HORROR IN MAINE

by Thomas Persano

Consultant: Debbie Felton
Professor of Classics
University of Massachusetts
Amherst, Massachusetts

BEARPORT PUBLISHING

Minneapolis, Minnesota

Credits

Cover, © Kim Jones, © Benjamin F Sullivan/Shutterstock, © John Gomez/Shutterstock, © NITIKAN TUMNITAYASAK/Shutterstock, © Angela N Perryman/Shutterstock, and © Rabbit_Photo/Shutterstock; 3, © cubart/Shutterstock; 4-5, © Kim Jones, © Mr.B-king/Shutterstock, © arburkholder/Shutterstock, and © CREATISTAShutterstock; 3, © Ken Morris/Shutterstock; 6, Wikimedia Commons/Public Domain; 7, © Allen Wood Photography/Shutterstock; 8, © Kiselev Andrey Valerevich/Shutterstock; 8-9, © Muratart/Shutterstock; 10, © Ulmus Media/Shutterstock; 10-11, © Trevor Fairbank/Shutterstock; 13, © Michael Ver Sprill/iStock and © Marko Aliaksandr/Shutterstock; 14, © Doug Kerr/flickr; 15, © Google Maps 2019; 16, © Rob Wilson/Shutterstock; 16-17, © JWCohen/Shutterstock and © Lario Tus/Shutterstock; 18, © Arisha Ray Singh/Shutterstock; 19, © Wangkun Jia/Shutterstock; 20, Courtesy Dick Shaw/Bangor Daily News/Public Domain; 21, © Travel Faery/Shutterstock and © Everette Collection/Shutterstock; 23, © Sunoloud/Shutterstock; and 24, © Flashon Studio/Shutterstock.

President: Jen Jenson
Director of Product Development: Spencer Brinker
Editor: Allison Juda
Designer: Micah Edel
Cover: Kim Jones

Library of Congress Cataloging-in-Publication Data

Names: Persano, Thomas, author.
Title: Horror in Maine / by Thomas Persano.
Description: Minneapolis, Minneapolis : Bearport Publishing Company, [2021] | Series: Scary states (of mind) | Includes bibliographical references and index.
Identifiers: LCCN 2020000583 (print) | LCCN 2020000584 (ebook) | ISBN 9781647470746 (library binding) | ISBN 9781647470845 (ebook)
Subjects: LCSH: Haunted places—Maine—Juvenile literature. | Ghosts—Maine—Juvenile literature. | Maine—Miscellanea—Juvenile literature.
Classification: LCC BF1472.U6 P4247 2021 (print) | LCC BF1472.U6 (ebook) | DDC 133.109741—dc23
LC record available at https://lccn.loc.gov/2020000583
LC ebook record available at https://lccn.loc.gov/2020000584

For more information, write to Bearport Publishing, 5357 Penn Avenue South, Minneapolis, MN 55419. Printed in the United States of America.

CONTENTS

Horror in Maine

Waves crash on the rocky coast along Maine's shore. Maine is both wild and spooky. Enjoy your time in its natural surroundings and historic towns, but be warned—you might not believe what you see!

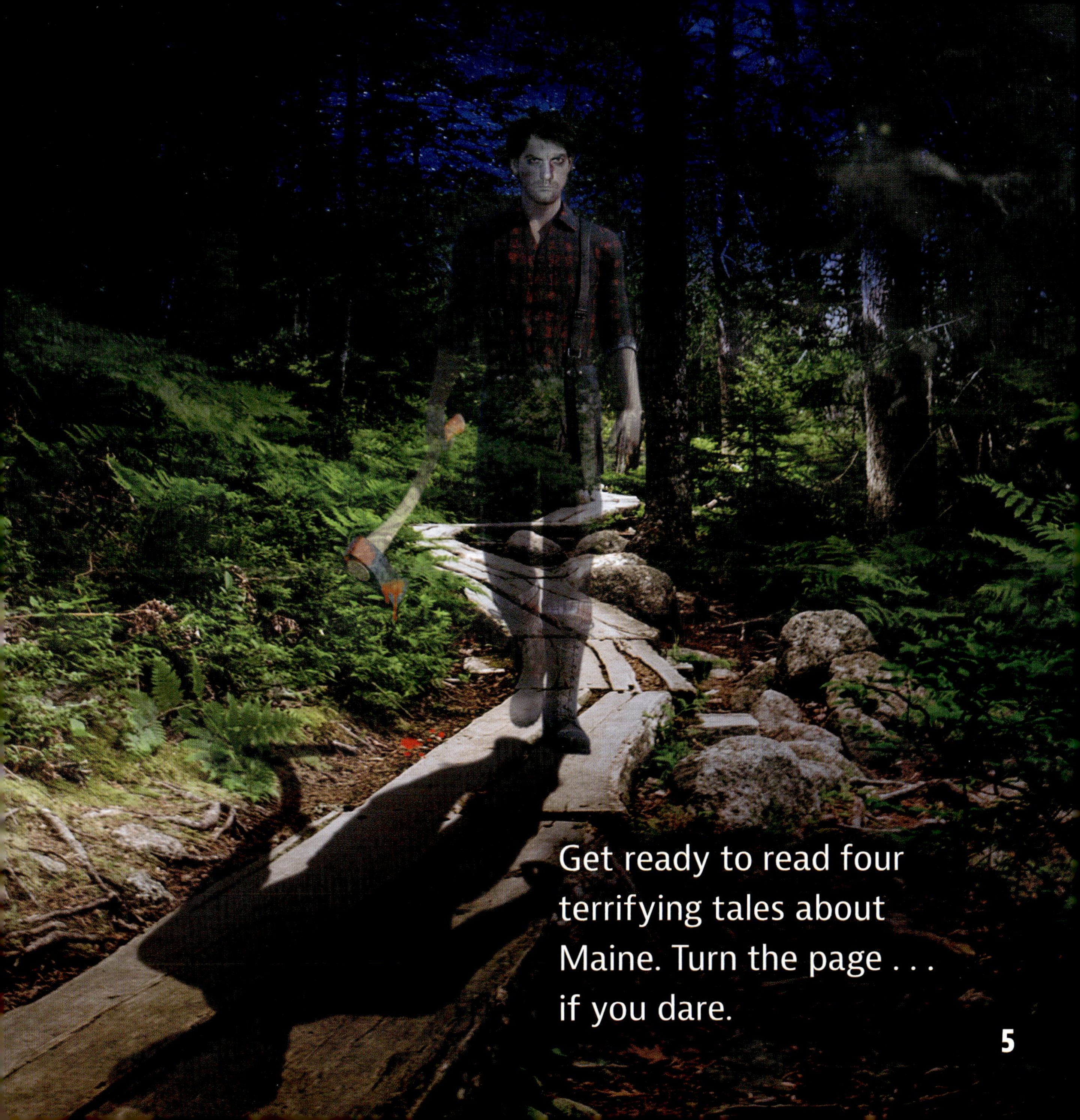

Get ready to read four terrifying tales about Maine. Turn the page . . . if you dare.

LONELY ISLAND

Boon Island Lighthouse, York

Boon Island is a **barren** and lonely place. The tall lighthouse on the island helps ships avoid the dangers along the rocky shores.

In the past, the lighthouse needed keepers to live on the island. It turned out to be a dangerous job not only for a keeper, but also for his wife.

Boon Island Lighthouse in 1911

The lighthouse on Boon Island is the tallest in New England.

During a terrible storm, keeper Luke Bright died. His wife, Katherine, bravely climbed to the top of the lighthouse to keep the light going for days. Later, sailors found her wandering alone on shore. She had gone mad from grief and soon died.

Visitors to the island say they've seen her ghost—still wandering and searching for her beloved Luke.

In 1710, a group of sailors was **stranded** on Boon Island after their ship sank. When they ran out of food, they started eating their fellow sailors.

CLOSE ENCOUNTER

Eagle Lake, Allagash

In 1976, four friends headed out for a fun fishing trip on Eagle Lake. What they got was an **experience** they would never forget!

The fishers were on their boats. Suddenly, they saw a fiery light in the sky above them. They tried to get away, but the light followed them.

Eagle Lake

The next thing they knew, they were back on the shore, and it was several hours later. They say they were taken onto a spaceship where aliens did **experiments** on them. Years later, the men still have nightmares about what happened on that lake.

The friends claim that many memories came back through the use of **hypnosis**. Some people think hypnosis doesn't work.

ROAD TO NOWHERE

Route 2A, Haynesville

Be careful if you drive along Maine's foggy, **winding** roads. Those who travel along Route 2A near the tiny town of Haynesville have seen a woman stranded on the side of the road. But when cars slow down to help, things get creepy!

Route 2A is very dangerous. The country song "A **Tombstone** Every Mile" is about the winding road.

The mysterious woman tells the helpful drivers there has been an accident, and her husband is hurt. If he doesn't get help soon, he might die! But when they begin to follow the women to help, she disappears! Is she a ghost trying to lead innocent people to their doom?

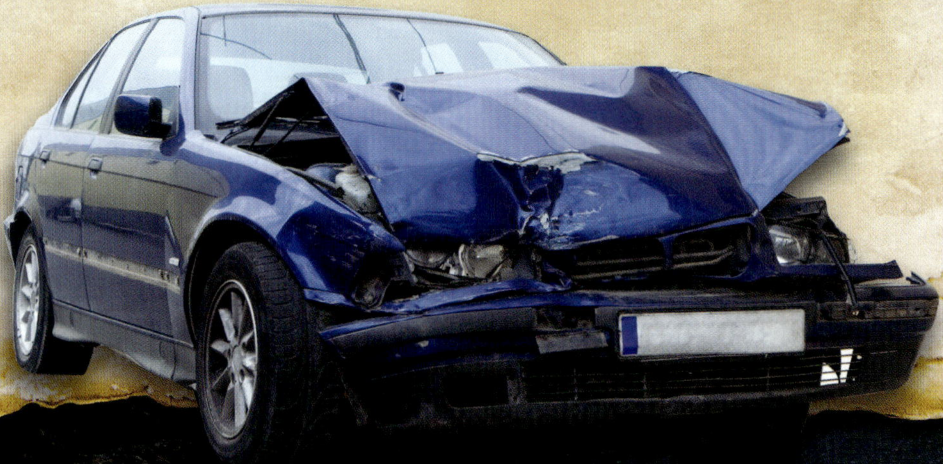

A NIGHT AT THE OPERA

Bangor Opera House, Bangor

People have been enjoying shows at the Bangor Opera House for many years. But not everybody who enters the opera house makes it out alive. In January 1914, firefighters tried to save the building from a raging fire. Two of them died when a brick wall fell on them.

Bangor Opera House

The opera house was rebuilt, but some performers and visitors have noticed a large, shadowy man standing in the balcony. He is wearing unusual clothes—almost like those an old firefighter would wear. Has this ghostly figure been standing there since the building burned down over 100 years ago?

The opera house just after the fire

Props and other objects at the opera house have gone missing or moved on their own. Workers think it might be the work of ghosts.

SPOOKY SPOTS IN MAINE

EAGLE LAKE
Keep your eyes on the sky at this remote lake.

ROUTE 2A
Will you help any stranded travelers on this haunted road?

BANGOR OPERA HOUSE
Visit a theater that has been haunted for over 100 years.

BOON ISLAND LIGHTHOUSE
Look into the distance to see a restless ghost.

GLOSSARY

barren (BEH-rin) empty

experience (ik-SPEER-ee-uhns) something that has happened

experiments (ik-SPER-uh-ments) tests to find something unknown

hypnosis (hip-NO-sis) a relaxed, trance state where people can recall lost memories

props (PROPS) objects used in plays

stranded (STRAN-did) left without a way to move from place to place

tombstone (TOOM-stone) a stone marking a person's grave

winding (WINE-ding) curving

INDEX

READ MORE

Camisa, Kathryn. *Ghostly Theaters (Tiptoe Into Scary Places).* New York: Bearport (2018).

Merwin, E. *Deserted Cities (Tiptoe Into Scary Places).* New York: Bearport (2018).

LEARN MORE ONLINE

1. Go to **www.factsurfer.com**
2. Enter "**Horror in Maine**" into the search box.
3. Click on the cover of this book to see a list of websites.

ABOUT THE AUTHOR

Thomas Persano lives in New York City. He has never seen a ghost in his life, but he wouldn't mind meeting a friendly one some day.